WHAT DO YOU Know!

LOST TO THE AGES

King Tut, Mayan Calendar, Extinction

Natalie Hyde, Jim Pipe, and Sonya Newland

A Crabtree Canopy Book

Crabtree Publishing
crabtreebooks.com

Authors: Natalie Hyde, Jim Pipe, and Sonya Newland
Editor: Kathy Middleton
Proofreader: Melissa Boyce
Design: Samara Parent
Production manager: Candice Campbell

IMAGE CREDITS

Dreamstime: Vladimir Korostyshevskiy, p 34 (top)

Library of Congress: p 12

NASA: NASA/ESA/STScI, p 41 (bkgd)

Public Domain: Harry Burton (1879-1940), p 5 (top); Harry Burton (1879–1940), p19 (top); p 43; Roelant Savery (1576–1639), p 58 (top); Tasmanian Archives, p 59

Shutterstock: agsaz, p 4; Jaroslav Moravcik, p 14-15; ANDY_DEN, p 16; Stella sophie, p 17; Andrea Izzotti, p 18 (bottom); LukeandKarla.Travel, p 20 (bottom); hemro, p 21; Patryk Kosmider, p 29; WH_Pics, p 31; Aleksandar Todorovic, p 34 (bottom); WH_Pics, p 35

Wikimedia Commons: One dead president, p 19 (bottom); Izapa Stela, p 37 (top)

All other images from Shutterstock

Crabtree Publishing

crabtreebooks.com 800-387-7650

In Canada: We acknowledge the financial support of the Government of Canada through the Canada Book Fund for our publishing activities.

Printed in the U.S.A./CP2025

Published in Canada
Crabtree Publishing
616 Welland Ave.
St. Catharines, Ontario
L2M 5V6

Published in the United States
Crabtree Publishing
347 Fifth Ave.
Suite 1402-145
New York, NY 10016

Library and Archives Canada Cataloguing in Publication
Available at Library and Archives Canada

Library of Congress Cataloging-in-Publication Data
Available at the Library of Congress

Hardcover: 978-1-0398-9766-3
Ebook (pdf): 978-1-0398-8179-2
Epub: 978-1-0398-8299-7

CONTENTS

CHAPTER 1

KING TUT

The Lost King

Lord Carnarvon hurried to Egypt from England. He carried with him a telegram from the **archaeologist** Howard Carter. It read: "At last have made wonderful discovery in Valley; a magnificent tomb with seals intact." Years of searching had finally paid off. They had discovered the tomb of the ancient Egyptian king Tutankhamun.

After days of digging through piles of stone **rubble**, they found a sealed door. Carter broke a hole in the plaster and peeked inside. What he saw by the light of his candle made him gasp. "Can you see anything?" Carnarvon asked. Carter replied: "Yes, wonderful things!"

Among the many beautiful treasures in Tut's tomb was a golden throne. On the back was a picture of the pharaoh and his wife.

Howard Carter and Lord Carnarvon at the door of the burial chamber.

An Interest in Egypt

Lord Carnarvon was an **amateur** Egyptologist from England. An Egyptologist is someone who studies the history and culture of ancient Egypt. In 1914, Lord Carnarvon got permission from the Egyptian government to dig in the Valley of the Kings. Many of Egypt's pharaohs, or kings, were buried there. Some archaeologists believed that all the tombs had been found. Lord Carnarvon thought they were wrong.

Carnarvon hired British archaeologist Howard Carter to look for new tombs. In earlier explorations, Carter had found clues that a pharaoh named Tutankhamun was buried in the valley. The young archaeologist was sure Tut's tomb was still hidden underground. But, by 1922, Lord Carnarvon was running out of money. He could only afford to pay the workers for one more season. Then Carter made his amazing discovery.

Today, we know that there are more than 60 royal tombs in the Valley of the Kings, near Luxor in Egypt.

This map shows some of the main sites in Egypt, including the Valley of the Kings, where Tut's tomb was found.

Who Was the Boy Pharaoh?

Ancient Egypt was ruled by pharaohs. A pharaoh was the political and religious leader of the land. The word "pharaoh" means "great house," which refers to the palaces where they lived. Both men and women could become pharaoh, but power was usually passed from father to son.

Tutankhamun's father, Akhenaten, died when Tut was young. His elder brother had also died. This meant that Tut was next in line to inherit the throne. He became pharaoh when he was only nine years old, in about 1332 B.C.E. Trusted advisers helped him rule Egypt while he was still a child.

A Royal Childhood

Tutankhamun grew up in the royal palace in the capital city of Amarna. As the son of a pharaoh, he had the best food and wore the finest linen clothes. He was cared for by nannies and educated in the "kap," or royal nursery.

The young prince received the best education. He was taught reading, writing, and mathematics. He spent many hours learning picture writing called hieroglyphics. He would make hieroglyphs on **papyrus** using a reed brush and ink. His ink palette was made of ivory and his name was carved into it.

The ruins of great palaces and temples built to honor the pharaohs can still be seen in Egypt.

Leisure Time

Life was not all about studying for the young Tutankhamun. On the hottest days, he went swimming in the nearby Nile River with his siblings and the children of other noble families. Nurses and guards stood on the shore, watching for dangerous crocodiles.

One of Tutankhamun's favorite pastimes was hunting ducks. A miniature bow, made to fit a child's shorter arms, was found in his tomb. Images in his tomb show him hiding in the reeds, stalking his prey. His sisters helped by passing him arrows.

Around the age of eight, Tutankhamun was taught to drive a chariot, which was a two-wheeled cart pulled by horses. His teacher helped him practice for weeks to control two lively horses over uneven ground.

This is Tutankhamun's royal name. Called a cartouche, the oval protects the name inside. The top three shapes stand for "Amun." The bird and two loaves of bread represent "Tut." The "Ankh" symbol beside it means life. The bottom symbols show he is the ruler.

Paintings often show Tut in his war chariot with his bow and arrow, fighting the enemy.

Kings of Egypt

To Egyptians, the pharaoh was more than a king. They believed their ruler was also a god. As well as running the country, the pharaoh had to keep the other gods happy with offerings and festivals. If he angered the gods, he could lose all his power. The pharaoh's main responsibility was to keep harmony, called Maat, within the country.

Sometimes keeping Maat meant going to war to protect Egypt's borders. Tutankhamun fought with the Nubian people who lived in the south. But mainly he tried to keep good relations with neighboring peoples. After a battle, the defeated country would pay a **tribute** of valuable items like gems or gold to the pharaoh.

Preparing for Death

The ancient Egyptians believed in an **afterlife**. Pharaohs spent most of their lives preparing for death. As soon as a pharaoh was crowned, work would begin on the ruler's tomb. The first pharaohs had small tombs in the ground covered by a brick building, called a mastaba.

Eventually, the mastabas became **pyramids**. Pyramids took thousands of workers many years to build. They were huge stone or brick structures, which could be seen from many miles away. This made them a target for tomb robbers, who wanted the precious objects that were buried with the pharaohs.

Tombs were built with hidden passages, trapdoors, or deep wells to confuse thieves. But this did not stop them. Often tombs were robbed by the men who built them. Some families were known as professional tomb robbers!

Later, pharaohs began looking for burial places that were more secret than pyramids to protect their tombs from robbers. The perfect place was discovered in a desert valley far from the Egyptian capital. Workers cut tombs deep into the canyon walls near the city of Luxor. They hoped this would make it harder for tomb robbers to find.

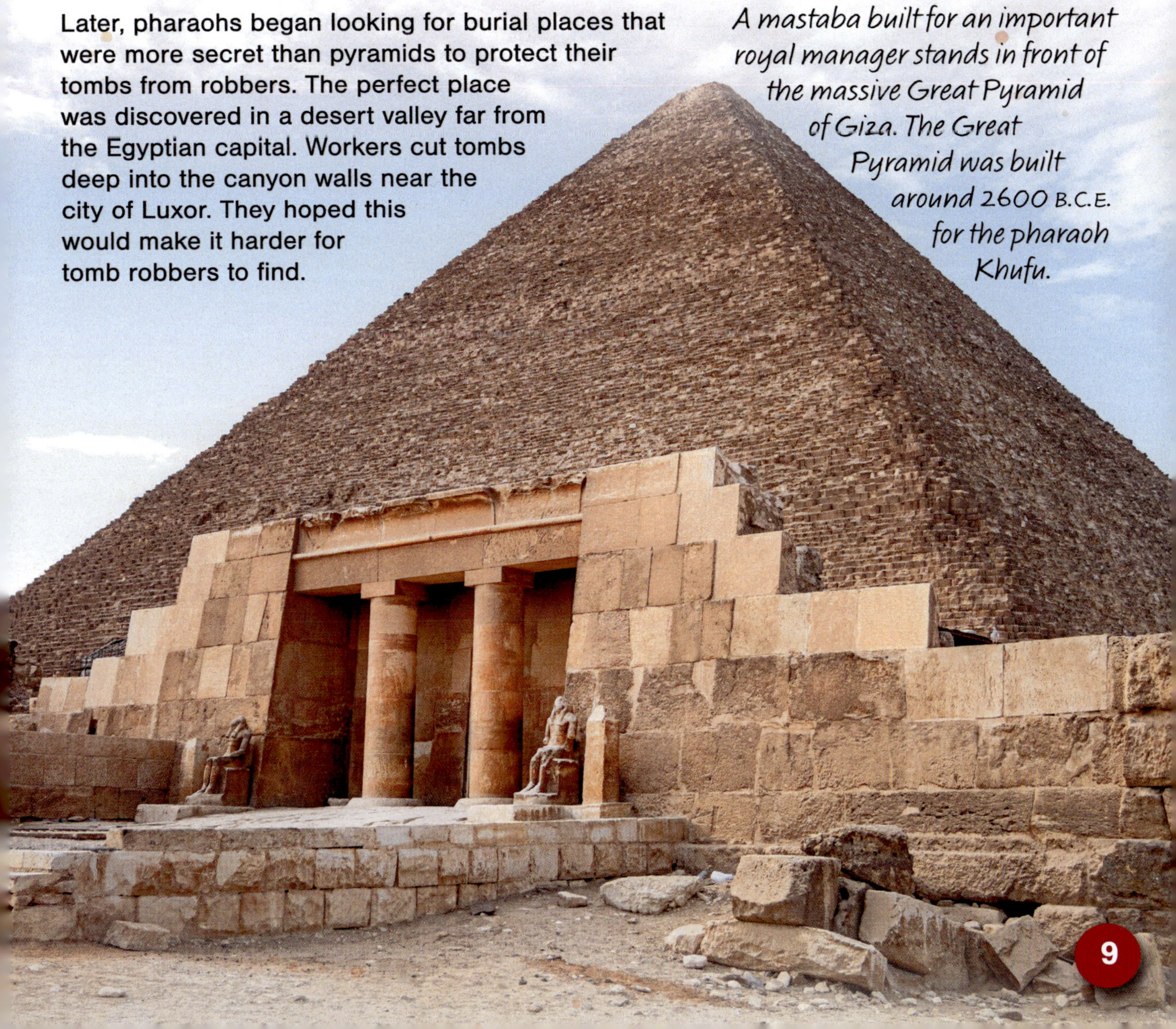

A mastaba built for an important royal manager stands in front of the massive Great Pyramid of Giza. The Great Pyramid was built around 2600 B.C.E. for the pharaoh Khufu.

The Valley of the Kings

This canyon is known today as the Valley of the Kings. The workers who built the tombs there lived in the nearby village of Deir el-Medina. A team of between 30 and 60 workers would dig, plaster, and paint a tomb in preparation for the pharaoh's death. Other important Egyptian men and women were also buried in the valley.

Tombs were built to hold all of the things the pharaoh would need in the afterlife, including his body. The walls and ceilings were decorated with scenes showing the gods helping the ruler on his journey after death. **Rituals** and prayers were also written on the walls. These were there to help the pharaoh move from death to his new life.

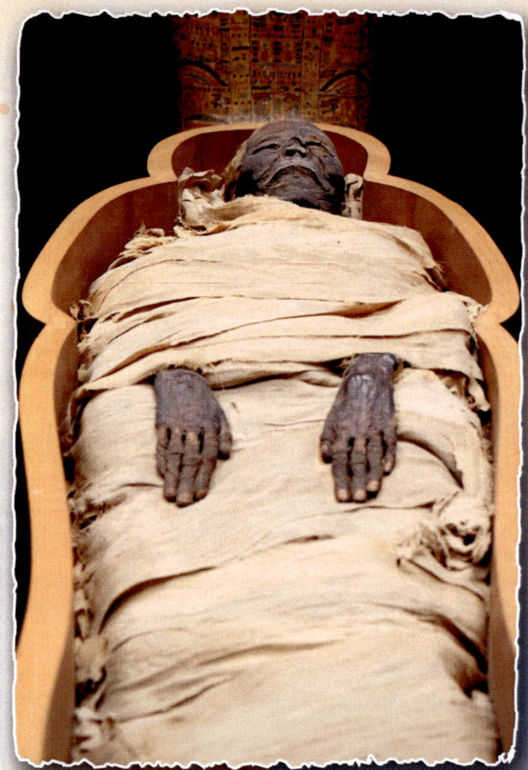

The bodies of the dead were carefully preserved with chemicals and wrapped in bandages.

Images of everyday life were painted on tomb walls. This image from a tomb shows a funeral procession. The dead person was often painted receiving offerings from others.

Packing for the Afterlife

In the tombs were all the things people thought the dead would need in the afterlife. Pharaohs were used to a life of luxury. They were buried with piles of valuable jewelry, furniture, and weapons. They also stored food, drink, and clothing for their new life.

Egyptians believed that they needed their body in the afterlife too. A mummy is a **preserved** body. The first bodies were mummified naturally in the dry sand of Egypt's deserts. Later, Egyptian priests learned how to use salt and chemicals to preserve bodies on purpose.

First, the priests removed important organs from the body. They put the stomach, liver, lungs, and intestines in special containers, called canopic jars. The lids were decorated with the heads of gods. Afterward, the dried body was wrapped in linen strips and placed in a coffin.

Canopic jars were made from limestone or clay. Each one held a particular organ such as the liver or lungs.

The village of Deir el-Medina, with about 60 houses, was home to the people who worked in the Valley of the Kings.

Finding Tut's Tomb

Tutankhamun was still only a teenager when he died in about 1323 B.C.E. His tomb was not yet ready for him. The priests needed to find somewhere that could be completed quickly. They chose a smaller tomb that was being built for a nobleman. After the young pharaoh was buried, the entrance was covered with rubble from a nearby tomb.

King Tut reigned, or ruled, for only a short time. There were few records left in Egypt of his life and deeds. Because his reign was unremarkable and his tomb was small for a pharaoh, people soon forgot the boy king's grave. While other tombs in the area were stripped of their precious objects, Tutankhamun's lack of fame protected his.

No one could believe it when the last gold ***sarcophagus*** *was opened, revealing the body of the boy king.*

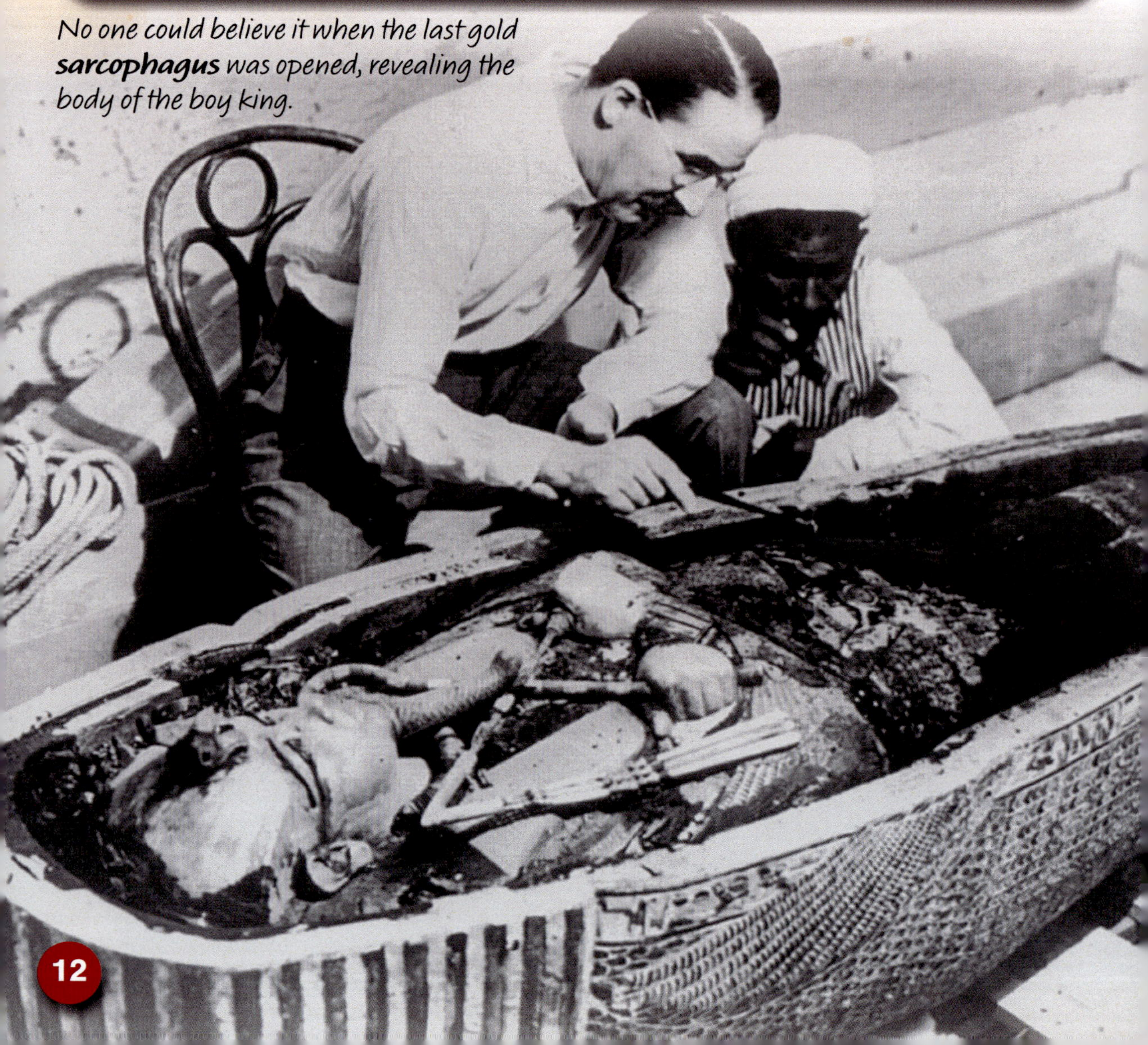

Carter's Big Find

Thousands of years later, Howard Carter and his team stumbled across Tut's tomb in the Valley of the Kings. They found the steps under the ruins of a worker's house. This discovery sent a wave of excitement around the world. The doorways were still sealed—perhaps some treasures survived in the darkness of this tomb!

Not even Carter and Carnarvon could have imagined the riches that actually lay behind those doors. Tut's tomb turned out to be the most **intact** Egyptian burial place ever found. Inside, items were piled from floor to ceiling in four rooms. There was hardly space for the archaeologists to squeeze in to work.

It was more than three months before Carter and Carnarvon were able to move enough objects to get to the burial room. The biggest question had still not been answered: was the mummy of Tutankhamun still inside? Or had it been moved or destroyed during the early robberies?

When they finally reached the burial chamber, they found it was almost completely filled by four golden shrines stacked inside each other. Shrines are boxes that hold sacred items. Beneath the shrines was a sarcophagus that held three coffins, also one inside the other. The last coffin was made of solid gold. Incredibly, the mummy of King Tut was still inside!

Today, the entrance to Tut's tomb is marked with a simple plaque with his name and the tomb number—62.

Tut's Treasures

The many items in Tutankhamun's tomb revealed an enormous amount about the life of the pharaohs in ancient Egypt. There were so many things crammed into the four small rooms that it took Carter 10 years to remove and catalog them all. In total, archaeologists found more than 5,000 objects.

Every item was numbered, described on a card, and photographed before it was removed from the tomb. Many of the **artifacts** were extremely fragile, or easily broken. Sometimes only a pattern of beads was left of a necklace. Some fabrics crumbled into dust when they were touched.

The Pharaoh's Furniture

Tutankhamun was buried with furniture for his new home in the afterlife. In the tomb were chairs, chests, and four beds. All were beautifully carved with animal heads and decorated with gold. Archaeologists could see that ancient Egypt had very skilled craftspeople.

Those who buried the young pharaoh made sure he would have fun in the afterlife too. There were several board games in the tomb, as well as many weapons for hunting. There were also six dismantled, or taken apart, chariots for him to drive in paradise.

The rooms in the tomb were piled high with all sorts of valuable objects, including jewelry, furniture, and statues.

"Details of the room within emerged slowly from the mist, strange animals, statues, and gold—everywhere the glint of gold."

Howard Carter

The King's Clothes

What can you learn from someone's clothes? Archaeologists could see from the size and shape of the 100 pairs of sandals that Tutankhamun had long, narrow feet. Also in the tomb were 139 canes. They looked like they had been used. This suggested that King Tut had problems walking.

Pharaohs and wealthy people in ancient Egypt wore a type of jewelry called pectorals. They wore them as brooches or as a necklace, like this one.

Gold, Silver, and Precious Jewels

In ancient Egypt, pharaohs wore a lot of jewelry. Jewelry was used as both decoration and as protection against evil spirits. Tutankhamun was buried with bracelets, earrings, necklaces, anklets, chains, and rings. These were made of pure gold and silver, **inlaid** with precious stones.

These everyday sandals were made out of papyrus, leather, and wood. Sandals found in Tut's tomb were made of wood and decorated with gold and bark.

Egyptian Art

Artwork and carvings on items in the tomb were like ancient photographs. The images gave archaeologists snapshots into the life of the boy king. Tutankhamun liked to hunt. Paintings show him in his chariot, hunting lions and ostriches, or squatting in the reeds hunting ducks.

Other pictures give us a glimpse into Tut's personal life. His golden throne is decorated with images of him with his wife, Ankhesenamun. She is gently **anointing** him with perfume. Other scenes show her handing him arrows while he hunted. They are shown as very fond of each other.

One wall of Tut's tomb was covered with pictures of him being guided by Egyptian gods and goddesses.

Tutankhamun had no intention of going hungry in the afterlife. There were 40 gallons (151 liters) of wine, and meat from geese, ducks, and oxen buried with him!

The Antiquities Service

Until the 1800s, artifacts from ancient sites in Egypt were not protected. Jewelry, statues, and even entire monuments could be packed up and shipped to other countries. In 1858, the **Antiquities** Service of Egypt was created. This government department passed laws to keep artifacts in Egypt.

Carnarvon and Carter had to hand over all the items they found. They would go on display in the Egyptian Museum in Cairo. Some people believe that Carter and Carnarvon smuggled some items out for themselves. Certainly, artifacts from the tomb have turned up in other countries.

The death mask from Tut's tomb is now one of the most famous and popular attractions on display at the Egyptian Museum in Cairo.

Touring exhibitions about Tutankhamun and Egypt's other pharaohs are popular all over the world.

Carter (left) and Carnarvon (right) did not believe in ancient Egyptian curses, but Carnarvon died within a few months of opening the tomb.

To discourage grave robbing, messages carved in stone were usually placed at burial sites. Messages, like this one, place a curse on anyone entering or stealing from the site.

Revealing Tut's Secrets

Ancient Egyptians believed that mummies were protected by spirits. A curse would fall on anyone who disturbed a grave or robbed a tomb. The curse might cause illness, bad luck—or even death. The curse was often written on the walls of the tomb as a warning to those who entered.

Howard Carter did not believe in curses. He ignored the warnings from local people and opened Tut's tomb. A few months later, Lord Carnarvon died from an infected mosquito bite. By 1929, 11 people from Carter's team had died. One of the dead was Richard Bethell, Carter's personal secretary. He was found smothered to death in his bed.

How Did Tut Die?

The discovery of Tutankhamun's mummy solved some mysteries, but it also created new ones. Scientists wondered what caused his death. Was he murdered? X-rays and special scans showed he had broken his leg in a fall. He also had **malaria**. These two things together may have killed him.

Modern science was also used to prove who Tut's parents were. DNA testing showed that his father was Akhenaten. His mother was traced to a female mummy found in another tomb. Her name is not known, but she was one of Akhenaten's sisters.

Advances such as DNA testing finally solved the mysteries of Tutankhamun's family tree. They showed that his father was the famous pharaoh Akhenaten, who worshiped only the Sun.

By studying his preserved body, scientists were able to find out a lot about this pharaoh who had died so young.

Tut Today

Some of the artifacts from Tut's tomb have been displayed on tours around the world. Millions of people have gazed upon the treasures of a boy king who lived more than 3,000 years ago. Forgotten for thousands of years, today, he is the most famous Egyptian pharaoh.

New Discoveries

Amazing discoveries are still being made in Egypt. Two new tombs were discovered in 2008 in the Valley of the Kings. One held five mummies but no grave goods. The other is the tomb of a royal court singer. New technologies such as **satellite imagery** may reveal the location of new pyramids, long buried by the sand.

The Supreme Council of Antiquities is trying to get back artifacts that were taken from Egypt long ago. Some have already been returned. One of these was a mummy displayed for many years at the Daredevil Hall of Fame in Niagara Falls, Canada. It was proven to be the mummy of the pharaoh Ramses I. The mummy was returned to Egypt.

Workers are still excavating in the Valley of the Kings. Who knows what treasures might still lie beneath the sand and rock?

CHAPTER 2

MAYAN CALENDAR

An Ancient Riddle

December 21, 2012, marks the final date of the last known Mayan calendar. Did the Maya believe that the world would end on this date? There is no **evidence** for this, but not everyone was convinced.

The Mayan calendar itself is like a giant puzzle. It is made up of several different calendars that fit together. We know how the Mayan calendar works, but not what it really means. People are still searching for clues to help solve this ancient mystery.

Over 1,000 years ago, the Maya were a powerful people. Their incredible knowledge of the stars, science, and mathematics still fascinates us today.

The Writing on the Wall

People have known about the Mayan calendar for hundreds of years. It is found in ancient books and in Mayan ruins. In 2011, archaeologists made an amazing discovery in Guatemala, in the ruined Mayan city of Xultun. It was a wall of a house that looked like a blackboard. The wall was covered in numbers. The numbers tracked how the Sun, the Moon, and the planets moved across the sky. The archaeologists figured out the meaning of the numbers. This was a 13-year calendar, the earliest one ever found written on a Mayan wall. This discovery helped unlock the mystery of how the Mayan calendar worked.

The Mysterious Maya

The search to uncover the mystery of the Mayan calendar begins in the thick, misty rain forests of Central America. More than 1,000 years ago, the Maya built great cities in what are now the countries of Mexico, Belize, and Guatemala.

Many magnificent Mayan buildings and **pyramids** can still be seen. They stand in places such as Tikal, Palenque, Copán, and Uxmal. The Maya are still there too. They are not a single people but many nations, sharing similar cultures, religions, and languages.

Paintings inside pyramids and in ancient books tell us about the Maya. They show holy **rituals** honoring the gods. The Maya believed there would be no crops without the help of the gods. They also thought their gods needed blood to grow strong. To feed the gods, Mayan priests killed enemies captured in battle.

The map below shows the main areas where the Maya lived.

For hundreds of years, Mayan cities were overgrown by the jungles of Central America. Some may still be undiscovered.

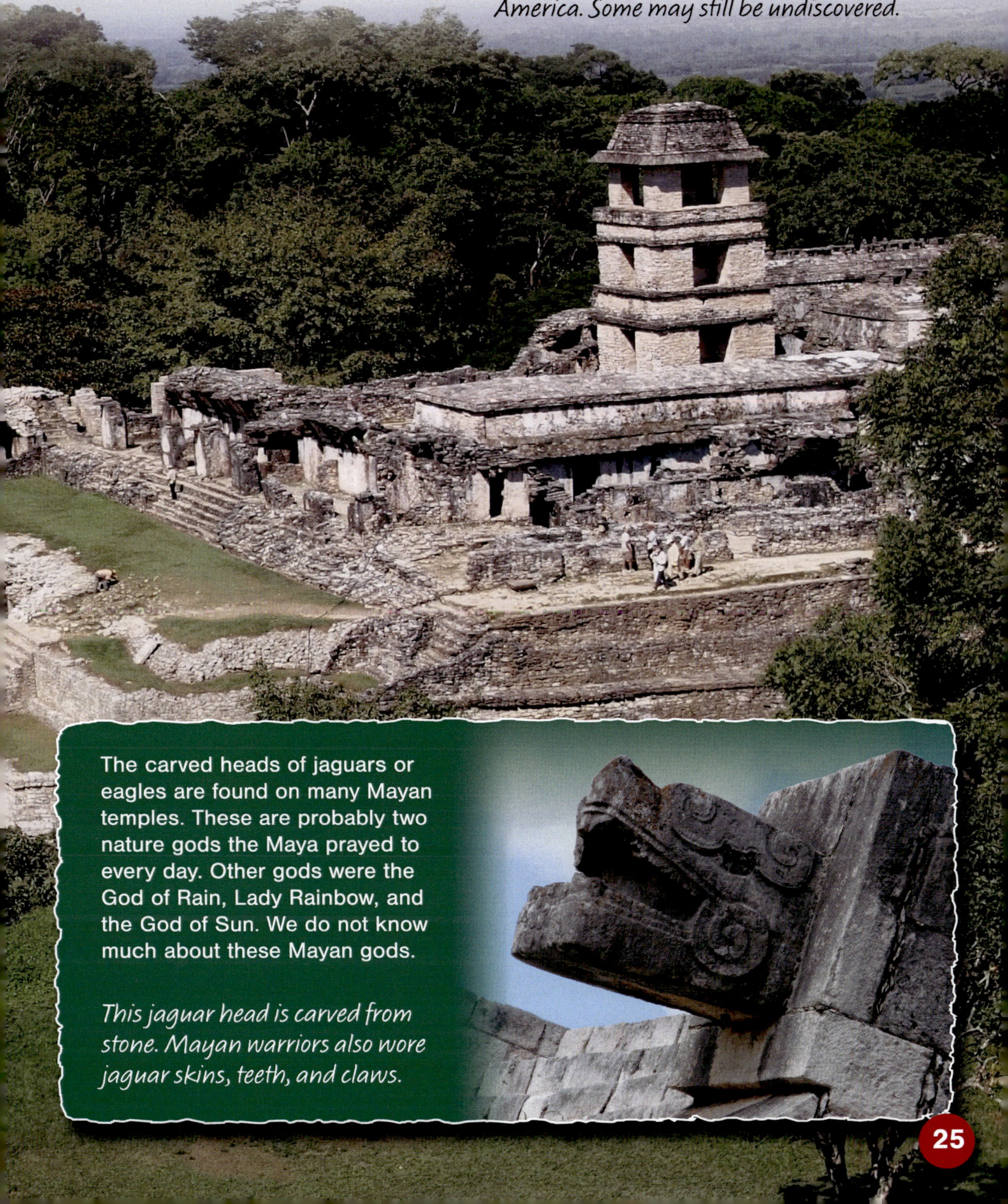

The carved heads of jaguars or eagles are found on many Mayan temples. These are probably two nature gods the Maya prayed to every day. Other gods were the God of Rain, Lady Rainbow, and the God of Sun. We do not know much about these Mayan gods.

This jaguar head is carved from stone. Mayan warriors also wore jaguar skins, teeth, and claws.

Palaces, Temples, and Tombs

The ancient Maya were also great builders. They built huge stone buildings such as palaces and temples. They buried their kings in large tombs. Most Maya were buried in their homes. This was so their relatives could still talk to them after they died.

Mayan priests looked to the stars to guide them. The Maya were skilled **astronomers**. They tracked the movement of the Sun, stars, and planets to choose lucky dates and predict the future. They did not have telescopes, so they may have used pools of water to reflect the night sky.

The Pyramid of the Magician at Uxmal towers over the rain forest. Some Mayan pyramids are over 200 feet (61 m) tall.

To the ancient Maya, spotting the planet Venus in the morning meant it was a good day for a battle.

Counting Time

The Maya were also very good at mathematics. They counted by sets of 20 instead of 10 as we do today. They could write large numbers using just three symbols. These symbols stood for zero, one, and five. Mayan astronomers used long calculations to figure out their calendars.

The Maya wrote down their history and what they saw in the sky in books called codices. These were made of soft tree bark. They folded like a fan. The Maya did not write using letters. Instead, they used about 700 little symbols called glyphs. The Dresden Codex is the most famous and most complete Mayan book ever found.

This Mayan codex shows some of the symbols they used for writing. Scientists still do not understand all the codex symbols.

Mayan numbers were made up of bars and dots.

Two Calendars

One Mayan calendar, the Tzolk'in, counted 260 days and was used to determine holy days. Another, the Haab, was a **solar** calendar. It counted 365 days per year. The Haab was used in everyday life. Each day had its own sign linked to plants and animals.

Time was very important to the Maya. Each day was a god. He or she carried the world and passed it to another god the next day. One day might be good for hunting. Another could be good for planting crops. Being born on the right date was very important.

There were also five unlucky days, which had no names. The Maya believed this was a time when the gods might cause disaster.

The Haab calendar had 18 months of 20 days, plus a short month of five days. These months are represented by the 19 glyphs in the circle.

Party Time!

The Maya celebrated events that happened every year. They also looked further ahead. Just once every 52 years, the Haab and Tzolk'in calendars ended at the same time. The Maya were happy to reach the end of this period safely. They celebrated with a big festival.

The festival was a time to make a fresh start. New layers were added to pyramids. Sometimes the Maya even lit huge bonfires to destroy their homes. Then they built them all over again.

The Maya celebrated with music, singing, dancing, and fire.

Clues to the End

The Maya believed that calendars could help them **predict** the future. Mayan predictions often warned of bad harvests or wars. Other **Indigenous** peoples of Central America have similar beliefs. They think the world is created and destroyed again and again.

The Aztec people of Mexico believe the world has actually ended four times. Destroyed by jaguars, a storm, a volcano, and a great flood, the world started over again each time. But did the Maya really believe the world would end completely?

Like the Tzolk'in calendar, the Aztec calendar counted 260 days a year.

Mayan rulers waited for a good day to fight a battle. They believed the gods could help them win.

Clue 1: The Long Count

When people talk about the Mayan calendar, they actually mean a third calendar, called the Long Count. The other two Mayan calendars—the Haab and Tzolk'in—marked regular events but not the years. The Long Count recorded every day in history for thousands of years.

How It Works

Each date in the Long Count calendar contained five numbers, for example, 4.5.4.3.1. Each number represented, or stood for, a grouping of a certain number of days. A mathematical calculation figured out how many days in total the date is from the beginning of the calendar.

The Long Count appears in the books of Chilam Balam, which means the "jaguar priest." These books were mainly written during the 17th and 18th centuries, long after the great Mayan cities disappeared.

Only four ancient Mayan books survive. The Madrid Codex is one of them.

Doing the Math

The largest number that can be created using the Long Count is 13.0.0.0.0. This is the same as 1,872,000 days or 5,125 years. So we know how long the Long Count lasts. But when did it start?

The Maya carved important dates on tall stone pillars called **stelae**. Several stelae show that "Day 1" in the Mayan Long Count was August 11, 3114 B.C.E. on our calendar. Adding 1,872,000 days to this gives us an end date of December 21, 2012.

This stela stands in the ancient Mayan city of Copán.

The Mayan rulers that appear on stelae often had strange names like "Smoke Monkey," "Fire-eating Serpent," and "Moon Jaguar."

The ancient Mayans carved their predictions in stone.

What did people expect would happen on December 21, 2012?

Our calendar is known as the Gregorian calendar. It was named after Pope Gregory XIII, who first used it in 1582. It repeats every 400 years.

The End of Days

After 13.0.0.0.0 there are no more days in the Long Count. This means December 21, 2012, is the final date in the Long Count calendar. This is why some people believed that the Mayan calendar predicted the end of the world.

Just because the calendar ends on this date, does not mean the Maya believed the world would end then. Most scientists think that the Long Count is more like the **odometer** in a car. If it ever reached 999,999, it would run out of numbers and simply go back to 0, starting all over again.

Round and Round

We know that the Maya believed things happened in a particular order. This is called a **cycle**. The cycle repeated itself constantly. So the final date of 13.0.0.0.0 in the Long Count may just mean that the calendar goes back to 0.0.0.0.1. Then it starts again.

Today, when we reach the end of the year on December 31, we start a new year on January 1. For many modern Maya, starting the Long Count again is something to celebrate too. They believe the whole world has a chance to make a fresh start.

It is more likely that the Mayan calendar represents a cycle of birth, death, and rebirth.

The number 13.0.0.0.0 on the calendar may also be the date that the Maya believe the world was created.

Modern Maya celebrate the start of a new year.

Written in Stone

Clue 2: Ancient Carvings

A strange stela was found in the ancient ruins at Tortuguero in Mexico. It describes something that was supposed to happen in 2012. This event involved Bolon Yokte. He was a Mayan god linked to both war and **creation**. The carving reads, “the god will come down from the sky.”

Another carving found on a brick at Comalcalco in Mexico is just as puzzling. Talking about December 21, 2012, it simply says “He arrives.” This carving was made about the same time as the one at Tortuguero. Perhaps they describe the same event.

Many Mayan gods were linked with destruction. The Maya believed that the Sun God Kinich Ahau sent his jaguars to Earth to eat humankind.

The stela from Tortuguero is damaged, and some of the words are missing. People are only guessing that the rest of the story is about the end of the world.

Alien Invasion

The Swiss writer Erich von Däniken said that the "god from the sky" meant an alien invasion. He claimed that aliens built the pyramids in Egypt and Stonehenge in England. Could this be what the Mayan carving meant?

In the last 60 years, there have been many false alarms about alien invasion. A report in 2010 warned that three large spacecraft heading toward Earth would arrive in 2012. The report claimed to have a photograph as evidence. The report was a **fake**. The spaceships were just blobs of dust on the photograph.

Some crop circles look like Mayan designs.

Sometimes strange shapes appear overnight in fields of crops. These flattened crops may look like landing sites for alien ships, but they are made by people using ropes and planks of wood as a joke.

A lot of people say they have seen alien spaceships in the sky.

Clue 3: Stela 25

Another interesting Mayan carving comes from the ruins at Izapa in Mexico. Here, Stela 25 shows a bird on top of a large tree. One **theory** is that this represents the Sun lining up with the center of our **galaxy**, the Milky Way.

Several Mayan carvings show the World Tree, which archaeologists think stood for the Milky Way.

Some people believed this lining up would happen when the Long Count ended. They thought it would cause terrible damage on Earth. There is no proof that the carving on Stela 25 really shows the Milky Way. Even if it does, we do not know that the Maya thought this meant the end of the world.

Our galaxy, the Milky Way, can be seen as a strip of stars and dust in the night sky.

Every year in December, Earth and the Sun line up with the center of the Milky Way. There have been no harmful effects so far!

Planets in a Row

Like the Maya, some people still look at the night sky to tell the future. Some suggested that on December 21, 2012, the planets might line up in a row. This could make the Sun wobble off center and tear itself apart.

This diagram shows what it would look like if the planets lined up. As far as we know, this has never happened.

Our Giant Sun

The pull between the planets and the Sun does make the Sun wobble, but only a little bit. This is because the Sun is so much bigger and heavier than the planets. The Sun's **mass** is more than 330,000 times greater than Earth's mass.

A giant **solar flare** could affect electricity on Earth, and even wipe out computer hard drives. This would be annoying, but not the end of the world!

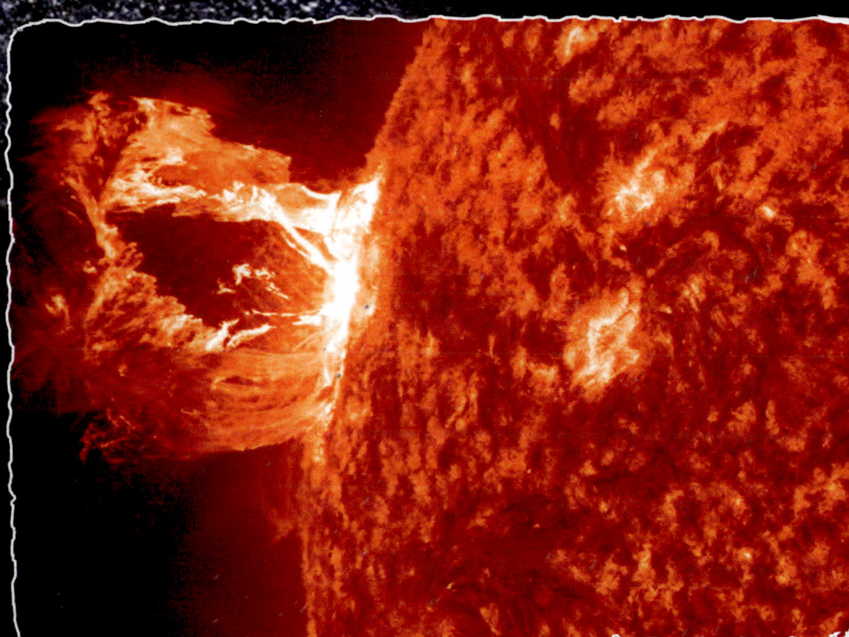

A huge solar flare shoots out of the Sun in April 2012.

Clue 4: The Dresden Codex

The Dresden Codex is a Mayan book. It contains calendars for different Mayan gods. It also contains tables about the Sun and the Moon. In the 1900s, the German scholar Ernst Förstemann pointed out that the last page of the codex showed a great flood.

Many cultures have flood **myths** that tell of the end of the world. Is this what the Maya meant? The flood picture in the book does not show people being washed away. There is no link between the Dresden Codex and the end of the Long Count.

> The Dresden Codex also includes the mysterious Serpent Number tables. Dates listed inside images of snakes go back to 34,000 B.C.E. The dates do not tie in with the Long Count calendar.

The last page of the Dresden Codex shows a great flood coming from the mouth of a dragon.

Many cultures around the world tell stories of ancient floods.

Tall Tales

Doomsday Stories

The Mayan calendar is still a mystery. No one knows if the Maya really predicted the end of the world. There are other doomsday stories, though. These have been inspired by the Mayan calendar, but most of them have nothing to do with the Maya.

Beware Planet X

Some people say that a wandering planet, called Niburu or Planet X, is heading toward Earth. Perhaps the Maya saw it too. Astronomers have found **dwarf planets** on the edge of our Solar System. But none seems likely to crash into Earth.

The dwarf planet Xena was first spotted in 2006.

A woman called Nancy Lieder said that aliens told her Planet X would pass Earth on May 27, 2003. Nothing happened!

If Planet X is real, this is what it would look like from the Moon.

Exploding Stars

Some people thought that the end of the Mayan calendar was a warning that Earth would be wiped out by a supernova. A supernova is a very old star that explodes. This creates a giant wave of energy. The wave rushes through space at 68 million miles (110 million km) per hour.

The red star Betelgeuse is set to explode in the next 100,000 years. No one knows exactly when it will happen. A supernova would need to be less than 50 light years away to threaten Earth, though. Betelgeuse is 640 **light years** away. If Betelgeuse did explode, the only effect on Earth would be a very bright star in the night sky.

This huge bubble of gas is the remains of a supernova. Appearing over 400 years ago, it is the last supernova seen from Earth.

"No star of that kind had ever shone before."

Astronomer Tycho Brahe, who saw a supernova in 1572

The End of the Ancient Maya

The greatest mystery is what happened to the ancient Maya. Around 900 C.E., they suddenly stopped building. Their great cities became ruins. Many Maya may have been killed by disease. Some experts think the Maya could not grow enough food to survive.

The Modern Maya

Maya people today still follow a calendar of 260 days. But they never believed the world would end in December 2012. For them, this date just marked the end of a cycle. Life began again afterward.

"The world will not end. It will be born again."

Carlos Barrios, a Mayan priest

The Maya god Quetzalcoatl was the master of life.

CHAPTER 3

EXTINCTION

Mass Extinctions

About 98 percent of all **species** that have ever lived on Earth are now extinct, or have died out completely. Most species survive for about 10 million years. Perhaps extinction is part of Earth's natural cycle. But when animals become extinct it affects us all and the world we live in.

Could something wipe out all life on Earth today? Could animals and humans be killed by an **asteroid** crashing into Earth? Could an erupting **supervolcano** or a deadly virus kill every living thing? Or will we end all life on Earth ourselves by exploding a nuclear bomb that would block out the Sun?

*The Sun will eventually become what is known as a **red giant**, before dying in a huge explosion.*

Scientists believe that all life on Earth will probably end in about 5 billion years. This is when the Sun will die. Without the Sun, nothing can live.

600 MYA	First animals emerge in the seas
450 MYA	Ordovician mass extinction
370 MYA	Devonian mass extinction
250 MYA	Permian mass extinction
230 MYA	First dinosaurs appear
200 MYA	First **mammals** appear
65 MYA	Extinction of the dinosaurs
70,000 YA	Humans nearly wiped out by volcano
10,000 YA	Woolly mammoths die out
1662	Dodo becomes extinct
1883	Quaggas die out
1896	Last passenger pigeons shot
1936	Tasmanian tiger becomes extinct
2011	Western black rhinoceros becomes extinct
2012	Last-known Pinta Island tortoise dies
2020	Splendid poison frog declared extinct

Life and Death

The first animals appeared on Earth about 600 million years ago (mya). Since then, millions of types of animals have become extinct. Some died out naturally over many years. Others were hunted to extinction by humans. More have died recently because of **climate change**.

Big Extinctions

Sometimes, many animals on Earth disappear at about the same time. This is what happened when the dinosaurs died out. The dinosaurs are not the only example, though. There have been at least five of these mass extinctions throughout Earth's lifetime.

The first mass extinction happened about 450 million years ago. It is known as the Ordovician mass extinction. At this time, there was just one continent on Earth. It slowly formed a huge area of frozen land.

The last Pinta Island giant tortoise, called Lonesome George, died in 2012.

Frozen Planet

Most animals lived in the sea. They died out as seawater turned to ice. There were only a few land animals. They could not survive the freezing temperatures of this cold new land. They died too. Two out of every three species became extinct.

Slowly, Earth warmed up again. New types of animals emerged on land and in the sea. The time in history called the Devonian period began. Another mass extinction happened during that period, 370 million years ago. Three-quarters of all species died.

Coral reefs were home to many sea creatures. The reefs were destroyed in the Devonian mass extinction. New ones did not grow for another 100 million years.

***Fossils** of trilobites have been discovered all around the world. These small marine arthropods were almost all gone by the end of the Devonian period.*

Death in the Sea

Scientists cannot connect the extinction with a single cause, but they know it affected sea animals the most. Even though they live in water, sea animals still need oxygen to breathe. But changes to Earth's climate meant there was not enough oxygen in the ocean any more. Only **bacteria** could survive there.

Lost World

The largest-ever extinction took place about 250 million years ago. This time was known as the Permian period. Plants and animals were very different to those around us today. Earth was covered in forests of giant ferns. Lizards the size of rhinos roamed the land.

Dimetrodon belonged to a group of animals called synapsids that lived in the Permian period.

Even great hunters such as the Tyrannosaurus rex did not survive this extinction event.

Huge plesiosaurs such as Elasmosaurus ruled the oceans during the Age of Reptiles.

The Great Dying

Suddenly, over 90 percent of life on Earth died out. This extinction was so terrible that scientists named it the "Great Dying." It may have been caused by huge volcanoes. When they erupted, they changed Earth's climate.

The most famous mass extinction is the death of the dinosaurs, 65 million years ago. It was not only the dinosaurs on land that died. Flying **reptiles** such as pterosaurs also died. Giant swimming reptiles such as plesiosaurs disappeared from the sea.

How on Earth?

The dinosaurs had been very successful at surviving. The time they lived on Earth is called the "Age of Reptiles" because they ruled our planet for 140 million years. Something very dramatic must have happened to make them extinct.

The Big Mystery

These mass extinctions happened a very long time ago. It is hard to know what caused them. Scientists spent many years trying to figure out what killed the dinosaurs. They came up with a lot of different theories.

Some dinosaurs were enormous. Perhaps they grew so big that they were crushed by their own weight. But animals do not grow so big that they cannot move! Also, if this idea was true then small dinosaurs would have survived.

Microraptor was a small dinosaur with wings. It was only about the size of a chicken.

The biggest animal ever to live on Earth is still alive. The blue whale weighs a huge 120 tons (109 metric tons). That is much more than any dinosaur.

Dinosaurs such as Diplodocus were huge, but they could still move about quite quickly.

Flowering Plants

For millions of years, only green plants, such as ferns, grew on Earth. Then plants with flowers began to appear. This was near the time that the dinosaurs died. One theory scientists had was that flowers may have been poisonous to the dinosaurs.

A dying star releases radiation that can travel through space. Could this be what killed the dinosaurs?

Star Explosion

Another early idea was that an exploding star killed the dinosaurs. When a star dies, it explodes. This is called a supernova. A supernova gives off a burst of **radiation**. Perhaps this radiation reached all the way to Earth, killing the animals.

The idea that flowers destroyed life on Earth does not make sense. Many sea animals died, and so did lots of plants!

Flowering plants appeared on Earth about 125 million years ago.

Diseased Insects

Another idea is that tiny bugs killed the dinosaurs. Some insects spread disease today. Perhaps biting flies made the dinosaurs ill. But scientists can tell from bones if dinosaurs had a disease. Not very many of them did.

Egg Thieves

Dinosaurs had been around for 30 million years before mammals appeared. The mammals were very small. How could they be a threat to the giant dinosaurs? Some people think that mammals ate all the dinosaur eggs. No eggs, no new dinosaurs. They could never have eaten them all, though!

Some dinosaurs also stole eggs from other dinosaurs' nests. The bird-like dinosaur shown here is an oviraptor. The name means "egg stealer."

Death by Volcano

Other theories about what killed the dinosaurs seem more likely. There was a huge range of volcanoes in India at the time of the dinosaurs. If some of them erupted together, it would have been a disaster for the planet's animals.

Erupting volcanoes would have pumped out smoke and dust. This could have poisoned the dinosaurs. It might also have changed the weather on Earth. Living things might not have been able to **adapt**.

When the dinosaurs died, sea levels were much higher than they are today. Changes in the weather could have caused huge floods.

Volcanoes may have released enough ash to block out the Sun. Living things need the Sun for survival.

Killer Asteroid

From the beginning, most scientists agreed that Earth changed just before the dinosaurs died. They just could not agree on why it happened. They also disagreed about how long the change took. Then, in 1980, a scientist named Luis Alvarez had a new idea.

Alvarez found evidence that an asteroid had smashed into Earth. The asteroid would have set forests on fire all over the world. It would have caused waves in the sea that were thousands of feet high. It would have sent up a huge cloud of dust, blocking out the Sun for months or maybe even years.

Earth might have been hit by a comet, not an asteroid. Comets are giant lumps of ice and rock in space.

An asteroid would have brought death to living things all over the world.

Effects of the Asteroid

Some animals would have been killed right away when the asteroid hit. Others would have died when their forest homes caught fire. With no sunlight, the planet would have become very, very cold. Dinosaurs were used to a warm, sunny Earth.

Plants cannot survive without sunlight. This means there would not have been enough food for plant-eating animals. As they died, the meat-eating dinosaurs that fed on the plant-eaters would have starved too.

Big Impact

The asteroid may have been more than 6 miles (9.6 km) wide. When it crashed into Earth, it was traveling at over 60,000 miles (96,560 km) per second. Such a huge impact would have left a **crater** 100 miles (160 km) wide!

No one knew yet where the asteroid might have struck. So the search began. Scientists all over the world began looking for a crater that was the right size. In the late 1980s, hidden under some younger rocks, the Chicxulub crater was found. It measures 112 miles (180 km) wide and 3,000 feet (914 m) deep.

The asteroid crashed into Earth so hard and so fast that it left an enormous crater.

The asteroid also released chemicals. These poisoned the water on Earth and caused **acid rain**.

The Chicxulub crater lies at the edge of the Yucatan Peninsula in Mexico.

The K-Pg Boundary

Scientists know about mass extinctions because of rocks and fossils. The end of the dinosaurs is marked by a layer of rock. Below this layer there are a lot of dinosaur fossils. Above the layer there are none. This is called the Cretaceous-Paleogene, or K-Pg, boundary.

Studying fossils can be difficult. Scientists do not often find the fossil of a whole dinosaur. Usually they find scattered bones. Dinosaur experts fit the pieces together like a puzzle. They have to guess about any missing pieces.

The Big Discovery

Luis Alvarez came up with his asteroid theory after studying rocks. He looked at rocks that formed at the same time as the dinosaurs died. Alvarez found some that contained a **mineral** called quartz.

The quartz was filled with cracks. Scientists call this "shocked quartz." The cracks had been caused by a huge explosion. The rocks also contained a substance called iridium. Iridium is very rare. It could only have come from space. An asteroid crash could explain both the shocked quartz and the iridium.

Luis Alvarez and his son Walter point out the K-Pg boundary in a layer of rock.

Occasionally experts make an exciting discovery—a whole skeleton preserved in rock.

After the Dinosaurs

Scientists believe it took the world 2 million years to recover from the asteroid impact. Gradually, the Sun warmed Earth again. New plants began to grow. Mammals, **amphibians**, reptiles, and insects spread across the globe.

The huge dinosaurs had been the kings of the planet. When they were gone, mammals took over. Five million years after the dinosaurs disappeared, the first large mammals appeared. There were more birds too, now that the giant flying reptiles were extinct.

This is a fossil of the first known bird, Archaeopteryx. It lived at the same time as the dinosaurs.

Mammals probably survived the asteroid crash because they were so small. They could burrow underground to stay warm and safe.

Mammals grew bigger and bigger. The huge horned Brontotherium was about 15 feet (4.5 m) long.

Disease has often been a threat to humans. In the 1300s, a disease called the Plague killed one-third of all the people in Europe and Asia.

Disaster Strikes Again

The death of the dinosaurs was not the last big extinction. Nature had more disasters in store. About 70,000 years ago, a supervolcano erupted in Indonesia. The ash blocked the Sun. The planet was plunged into a winter that lasted 10 years.

Human Extinction?

Even after the ash cloud cleared, temperatures on Earth stayed cold. Humans struggled to survive. Many did not. In the end, there may have been only about 2,000 people left in the whole world. If there had been one more disaster or a terrible disease, humans might have become extinct.

Lake Toba in Indonesia lies in the crater of the supervolcano that erupted thousands of years ago.

Woolly Wipeout

Humans survived the supervolcano's supereruption. They also survived the last **Ice Age**, which ended about 10,000 years ago. Many animals were not so lucky. Woolly mammoths, woolly rhinos, and saber-toothed tigers all died out about the time of the last Ice Age.

New Threats

Early humans may have speeded up this extinction. They hunted the animals for food. In Australia, there were giant kangaroos and enormous lizards called Megalania. Both animals were hunted to extinction.

The dodo could not fly, so it was an easy target for animal and human hunters.

A few woolly mammoths survived on an island in the Arctic until about 3,700 years ago.

Most experts think that the change in Earth's weather killed these large mammals. They fed on grasslands, which disappeared as the world got warmer and trees began to grow instead.

Hunted to Extinction

Humans have always hunted animals. At first, people caught animals for food or to make clothes from their fur. Later, humans hunted for sport. In the past few hundred years, people have caused many animals to become extinct.

Dead as a Dodo

Flightless dodo birds lived on the island of Mauritius for 2 million years. Then people arrived. Within 100 years, they had killed all the dodos. Many other birds have been hunted to extinction. In 1896, hunters killed the last flock of passenger pigeons.

The very last Tasmanian tiger died at a zoo in 1936.

> *"The extermination [death] of the passenger pigeon meant that mankind was just so much poorer."*
>
> *U.S. President Theodore Roosevelt*

The Future

Plants and animals in Earth's **ecosystems** depend on each other. If a plant or animal dies out, the animals that rely on it for food or shelter will also die. Animals that eat other animals are important too. They keep the numbers of certain species down so they don't eat all the food.

Humans are the greatest threat to life on Earth. For example, we cut down forests and clear land for farming. This destroys the homes of many animals. Some have not been able to survive.

In 1987, there were 1,500 golden toads left. Two years later they were extinct. Today, toads and frogs are facing a mass extinction, caused partly by human activity and partly by a deadly disease.

More than half the world's forests have now disappeared, most of them in the last 50 years.

A Changing World

Gases released from cars and factories also harm the planet. They cause the whole world to warm up. Eventually this might cause violent storms or turn the land to desert. Climate change is already affecting many animal species.

Going, Going, Gone

Between 20,000 and 2 million species have become extinct in the past 100 years. The rate of extinction is getting faster too. More than 17,000 species are at risk of becoming extinct. How many of these animals will die out in the next 100 years?

"It is not the strongest of the species that survives, not the most intelligent that survives. It is the one that is most adaptable to change."

Charles Darwin

It is getting warmer at the North Pole. As the ice melts, animals such as polar bears find it harder to live and hunt there.

GLOSSARY

acid rain Rainwater that contains harmful chemicals

adapt To develop different features to survive in new conditions

afterlife Life after death

amateur Someone who does something as a hobby, not a job

amphibians Egg-laying animals that live on land and in water

anointing Blessing someone, usually with oil or perfume

antiquities Objects from ancient times

archaeologist A scientist who studies ancient cultures

artifacts Objects made by people in the past

asteroid A lump of rock and metal that moves around in space

astronomers Scientists who study objects in space

bacteria Tiny creatures made of a single cell

climate change Changes in the weather over a long period of time

crater A bowl-shaped dip in the ground

creation The beginning of the world

cycle A group of events that happen over and over again

dwarf planets Small, round objects that move around the Sun

ecosystems All the plants and animals in particular areas

evidence Proof that something has happened

fake Something that has been made up

flightless Birds that live on the ground because they cannot fly

fossils The remains or impressions of animals and plants that died long ago

galaxy A group of billions of stars, dust, and gas in space

Ice Age A long period when Earth's climate is very cold

Indigenous The first inhabitants of a place

inlaid An item that is set into the surface of another object

intact Not broken or touched in any way

light years The measure of how far light travels (about 6 trillion miles (10 trillion km) in a year)

malaria A disease spread by mosquitoes that causes fever

mammals Warm-blooded animals that give birth to live young

mass A measure of the amount of matter in an object

mineral A solid natural substance that has a crystal-like shape

myths Traditional stories

odometer A device that measures how far a car has traveled

papyrus A type of paper made from the stems of reed plants

predict To work out what will happen in the future

preserved Kept in its original condition

pyramids Solid shapes with four steep sides that meet at the top

radiation Energy that can be harmful to living things

red giant A star that has burned all the hydrogen in its core and grown much larger in size

reptiles Cold-blooded animals that lay eggs

GLOSSARY

rituals Holy or special ceremonies to mark particular events

rubble Pieces of stone left over from a building

sarcophagus A large, decorated stone coffin with smaller coffins inside

satellite imagery Pictures taken from space

solar Based on the cycle of the Sun

solar flare A bright burst on the Sun's surface

species A particular type of animal or plant

stelae Tall slabs or stone pillars used to mark important events

supervolcano A giant volcano

theory An idea that has not yet been proven true

tribute A gift made to show respect

LEARNING MORE

Books

Howell, Izzi. *The Genius of the Maya: Innovations from Past Civilizations.* Crabtree Publishing, 2020.

Howell, Izzi. *Go Quiz Yourself on Dinosaurs.* Crabtree Publishing, 2021.

Kerry, Isaac. *Inside King Tut's Tomb.* Lerner Publishing Group, 2023.

Loureiro, Stephanie. *Animal Extinctions: A Graphic Guide.* Graphic Universe, 2024.

Newland, Sonya. *The Genius of the Ancient Egyptians: Innovations from Past Civilizations.* Crabtree Publishing, 2020.

Spilsbury, Louise and Sarah Eason. *The Maya: Fearsome Fighters and Scary Sacrifice.* Cheriton Children's Books, 2023.

Websites

https://tinyurl.com/4jx49b28
National Geographic shares the treasures found in the tomb of King Tutankhamun.

https://historyforkids.org/ancient-egyptian-architecture/
Get the facts on ancient Egypt's architecture.

www.history.com/topics/maya
Interesting videos from the History Channel about the Mayan civilization.

https://tinyurl.com/2uaaw9rn
Fascinating information about the Mayan calendar.

https://tinyurl.com/7hrxhwpb
Read about scientists trying to bring back the Tasmanian tiger from extinction.

https://www.amnh.org/explore/videos/shelf-life/six-extinctions
Watch a video about mass extinction from the American Museum of Natural History.

INDEX